MW01121074

Without

Instructions

R. A. D'ARCHE

WESTBOW
PRESS®
A DIVISION OF THOMAS NELSON
& ZONDERVAN

WestBow Press books may be ordered through booksellers or by contacting:

WestBow Press
A Division of Thomas Nelson & Zondervan
1663 Liberty Drive
Bloomington, IN 47403
www.westbowpress.com
1 (866) 928-1240

ISBN: 978-1-5127-5986-0 (sc)

Library of Congress Control Number: 2016916869

Print information available on the last page.

WestBow Press rev. date: 10/14/2016

Foreword

The pages before you will affect your life, or at least offer some clarity when looking back on how you have lived. What you will read may even broaden your perspective on navigating your future. Hopefully, you will choose to live life to its fullest and reflect deeply on the people and the events that not only shape your life but also occupy a permanent part of your soul.

Ray D'Arche has lived a life full of various events that have changed the course of his being. He has overcome great obstacles and has won even greater victories. Among his many accomplishments as a hard-working man, he is best known by his family and friends as a devoted and loving father who always puts his loved ones before himself. Now at age 84, Ray will always be remembered as a well-known and skilled craftsman. Following in his father's footsteps, he continues to be one of the oldest men in the State of Connecticut to maintain a Master's License in all three trades of plumbing, heating, and electrical. His life-long customers loved him for his honestly and integrity, talented and skilled mind and constant dedication and commitment to excellence in everything he was involved with. Some of Ray's closest customers became some of his most beloved friends. It was these customers who joined his family in knowing what most did not; that behind his weathered hands and stained work clothes he was an artist and writer of poetry. On a typical hot summer afternoon, Ray would spend time in between scheduled appointments either pulled over in his van or in his favorite restaurant parking lot, deep in thought while pondering his next words. He would often operate on impulse, capturing and crafting his words on the fly wherever and whenever he could. Most of the time his pen would fill all available space on anything he could find; napkins, bags, receipts, bills, an occasional notepad and even on the inside of his palm. At times, his young apprentice and "helper on the side" would stare as Ray puffed a cigarette deep in thought while ignoring his AM radio, and even watched tears stream down his face while he wrote. He would turn to that young man and explain the importance of catching words before they escaped the mind, no matter what.

Today, remembering that lesson is more important than ever. I ought to know. I was that young man watching him write. Today, I am his very proud son. Before you is a collection of Ray's most heartfelt work; a reflection of his life as a craftsman, father, husband and friend to many. His work continues to touch the lives of countless individuals who are astonished still to this day by the impact of his words.

With much love and gratitude,
Steve

Dedicated To

The following writings are dedicated to Jesus Christ my Lord and Savior, Jane McDonald Badgley, Perry Corlis Badgley and their daughter Carol Badgley D'Arche.

<u>Carol</u>

She has worked as a bookkeeper, teacher, secretary, caregiver to the elderly, part-time bus driver and full-time homemaker.

She has a relentless source of energy, an infinite amount of compassion and a eternal fountain of love.

She is purity and sweetness, God's work at its best; my adorable, devoted and loving wife.

R. A. D'Arche

Without Instructions

You came to this world, a child so small
Without any notes or instructions at all,
So we started from scratch, the best we knew how
And promised to God this one sacred vow.

> We vowed as your parents to give you our love
> And asked for God's guidance from heaven above,
> We asked that our love would always show care
> And judgment by us would always be fair.

You started to crawl, then started to walk
And before we knew it, you started to talk,
You started to run, then started to play
Then off to school, you started one day.

> We vowed as your parents to help you do right
> And said prayers to God each morning and night,
> We asked for the wisdom to teach you the truth
> To make your ways strong at the start of your youth.

You grew from a youth to quite a young lad
The years went by quick, too quick we might add,
Then in a twinkle your youth was all done
You had come to the age of a man twenty-one.

> We vowed to our God thru all of those years
> To love and to keep you thru smiles and tears,
> We asked for His help until you were grown
> And out in the world and all on your own.

So now you are grown, the teaching's complete
Each path that you walk will be by your feet,
But if you need help as you go on the way
It's best to remember we taught you to pray.

> We vowed to our God when roads were too bent
> To pray even more for answers He sent,
> And God answered our prayers, answered each one
> He gave us this man we're proud to call son.

What Brought You

God picked a lovely flower
From His garden wall
And sent it as an answer
To a very special call.

He sent it to your parents
He sent it down to earth
He gave it love and life
Dear child it was your birth.

You are a special flower
Born of Eden's land
Picked for Mom and Dad
By God's own loving hand.

And the reason you were picked
Was because God wisely knew
That the love which gave you life
He saw as really true.

You have been blessed with beauty
Delivered by God's own dove
But remember throughout life
What brought you here was -- love.

A Mother To Her Son

I helped you from your crib,
I taught you how to pray.
I tied your little bib
I loved you night and day.
I tucked you into bed,
I watched you as you ran,
And so the days have fled
From babe to boy to man.

And now that you must go
A road away from me,
I want to let you know
The love I have for thee.
I miss the babe in you
That once was only mine,
But love the boy that grew
Into a man so fine.

Dear Mom

Remember that big yellow bus
That came early for me one day?
And how, with my hair you did fuss
Just before it took me away?

>   I too, remember that past,
>   The day that dust blew in your eye
>   And though it didn't seem to last
>   It caused you, dear mother, to cry.

Remember the day when your boy,
Said vows of his faith before all?
You smiled and laughed with such joy
So proud of this little guy, tall.

>   I too, remember well that day
>   It's what you called a happy high
>   Yet even now I still must say
>   It caused you, dear mother, to cry.

Remember, the time, just last year
When high school days were finally done?
And then again there was a tear
The pride of mother for son.

I too, remember well you see
But now I know the reason why
It's all the love you have for me
That caused, you dear mother, to cry.

Remember with tomorrow's day,
The yellow bus comes back for me?
And even though I've gone away
I know the tears that I will see.

The tears of joy and pride and love
Will trickle down your cheeks for me,
I thank my Lord and God above
For this His gift, my memory.

I love you mom, I always will,

-- your son --

Grains Of Sand

I was up in the attic a week ago last
To clean and discard some things of the past.
And there in the corner I found a brown bag
I thought for a moment was just an old rag.
But as I reached down I saw a bright string
Was firmly attached to the top of this thing.
And as I unfolded this brown paper sack
Tears came to my eyes as memories went back.
I remembered the gift of this bag full of sand,
And the note that was printed by your six-year-old hand.
In a verse from the past I had long since forgot
I read those dear words you wrote as a tot.
"Much more than each grain of sand that you hold
Is how much I love you and more when you're old."
O sweet little child you now are full grown
But one day you'll have a child of your own.
So I'm writing in hopes that you'll save some small part
Of gifts that will come from your child's heart.
For there is nothing more dear that a mother could hold
Than the memories of love when she has grown old.

Blessings

I wish that I could have
A talk with God today,
And have Him tell me why
He took my friend away.

He took him from his wife
'And his dear children too.
I cannot understand
Why God this thing would do.

I know my friend would say
God reasons not for me,
And when I learn to trust
Then God will let me see.

And just today I learned
The suffering of my friend
It was a blessing true
His life had come to end.

My friend believed in God
His life did end to show
That when you truly trust
From God all blessings flow.

Upon My Bended Knee

When I was just a babe,
I heard my mother pray
To God in heav'n above
And this is what she'd say.

"On bended knee I bow
Before the Lord this day,
I pray that you will keep
This babe from all harm's way."

When I was still a boy,
My mom she was the one
Who thanked the Lord above
As every day was done.

"On bended knee this night
To thee I bow my head,
And thank you for my boy
Who rests so safe in bed."

When I became a man
I'd visit now and then,
And when I saw her last
I heard her pray again.

"On bended knee I ask
You help this man be strong,
For I have heard your call
And I will be along."

The years have swiftly flown,
My mom's no longer near
Yet somehow I still sense
A prayer I know I hear.

"On bended knee I come
Before the Lord to say,
Please grant a mother's wish
And teach my son to pray."

Lord give my mother peace
And tell her just for me,
That I have prayed to you
Upon my bended.

The Book of Life

Each life is like a book it's said,
That God will sit and read one day,
The story of the life we've led
Is written by our traveled way.

No matter how for man you act,
Your living scribes what's really true,
The book will have the truth of fact
About the life that's really you.

Thus let your book of life be bound
As though man were to see as God,
And when the Lord, your book has found
He'll smile upon the path you've trod.

A Child Shall Lead

I took my son, on Easter day
Down to the church to let him pray.
I do this so my son can be
As proud as he should be of me.
So to the church we walked that day
And as we did I heard him say
What he had learned in Sunday school
About the Lord of golden rule.
But then he looked at me and said
That he had learned God's son was dead.
But then God made him well again
And sent him back to live with men.
I shook my head and said – not true
That's just a story like 'Boy Blue'.
It's told to help the weak feel free
It's not for men like you and me.
And then he said in tone so weak
He'd rather be among the meek.
I turned to him with angry voice
And told him that he had no choice!
Don't ever let me hear that whine
From any boy that I call mine.
I saw him wince, then bite his lip
And then he pulled away my grip.
I knew I'd hurt this little guy

Who couldn't understand the why
But after church I'd tell him kind
That heaven and hell was in the mind.
But now, in church, was not the time
Besides the bells began to chime.
And then the pastor rose to say,
Please bow your heads and let us pray.
The pastor looked at my young son
And then the sermon was begun.

He spoke of Thomas, Lord's best friend
Who didn't believe until the end.
But as he spoke a dream began
That took me far from earth and man.
It took me to a time and place
Where there he stood, the Prince of grace.
Oh ye of little faith, He said
Why doth thou think that I am dead?
For surely you can see that I
Am Lord of all the earth and sky
Come place your hand within my side
And you will know just how I died.
And as I reached to feel the place
I felt the tears upon my face.
My hand was stuck within His side

'Twas then I knew that I had died
Release me from my sins I pray
And give me life just one more day.
And as I prayed these words of fear
A voice did whisper in my ear.
The Lord shall send from His great land
A child to lead thee by hand.
The vision faded from my sight
But still my had 'twas holding tight.
And when my sight came back to be
My son was standing next to me.
He held my hand and asked me why
I had a tear within my eye.
I bowed my head in thankful prayer
For now I knew that God was there.
I'm not quite sure of my reply
I only know I didn't lie.
But as we left that Easter day
It was my child that led the way.

Easter 1990

The Dearest of All

Of wishes three that God does give
Is love and children and life to live.
And within this gift, for man of life
He gives to him a loving wife.
And unto woman God did impart,
A home and house for a second heart.
Then to share between the two,
He gives a life to start anew.

Thank you God for the gift of three
And thanks for the life you've given to be.
Thanks for the children you sent from above,
And thanks for this family so full of your love.
But of all the things God gave to me,
The dearest of all was His gift of thee.
Thanks be to God that He gave me your life,
And thank you my dear, for being my wife.

My Valentine

I have failed at things a few
But never in my love for you.
Yet more success I'll never see
Than in the love you've given me.
And, the greatest joy of my life
Is knowing always, you're my wife.

Happy Valentine's Day 1993

The List

I started to make a list out today
Of all the good you have sent my way.

Love was, of course, at the top of the list
And surely kindness was not to be missed.

Giving and forgiving it was there too
Understanding warmth that surely was you.

You have given to me a wonderful life
And happiness too, by being my wife.

Now at the end and looking over this list
I noticed the most important was missed.

It is the total of all the other
It is your gift of being a mother.

Happy Mother's Day!

From The Heart

It was just before the dawn
Of Merry Christmas day –
Behold, the angel of gifts,
She was walking toward my way

I knew that she'd be coming
To wave her wand of grace –
I laughed and then I chuckled
As smiles lit my face.

Now, at last, my friend would know
Just why I gave so much.
I spent a lot of money
To earn this angel's touch.

Too bad, I thought, my poor friend
That you can't spend like me
But after all that I am worth
I know you would agree.

Blessed it is to give, not get
I smile now even more –
For my friend can't eve'n afford
A wreath upon his door.

My door I now, open wide
To let the angel through –
'Tis when I found my friend's note
That said "may God bless you."

Then I saw the angel pass
And go to my friend's place -
Raising up her wand of love
She blessed his house with grace.

And as the spirit left me
It said to me in part –
"…Remember that in giving
It must come from the heart."

(Christmas 1989)

Live His Way

Success is not for you
To give or take from me,
Success is not a gift
Nor is it ever free.

Success is not the wealth
That man may pile high,
Success is not a rank
For which you bid and vie.

Success is what you earn
From God this very day,
It is a loving peace
For those who live His way.

The Right Gift

'Twas two nights before Christmas,
My shopping was done,
Each gift was all wrapped,
A name on each one.

The gifts were all chosen
So all could quite see,
That cost was no object
When the gift came from me.

But then came a feeling
I can't quite explain,
And tears on my cheeks
Were flowing like rain.

I knew in an instant
That each wonderful gift
Was in some way still lacking
That magical lift.

I thought of the spirit
That Christmas time brings
'Twas then that I knew
It was not in these things.

So back to the store
I went thru the night,
All gifts must go back
They just were not right.

I waited a day
To think this thing thru,
Yet still in a quandary
There was naught I could do.

'Twas the night before Christmas,
My gifts were all gone;
My friends would be coming,
Just after the dawn..

I went for a walk
To ponder this thing
And that's when I heard,
A little bell ring.

I turned right around
And I saw a mans face
He was ringing a bell
A pot by his place

I knew in a moment
Each gift that I'd send.
I took all my money
And gave for each friend.

A letter to Diane

Dear Diane –

God has taken your dear husband neither I nor anyone else I know could give you a reason that could possibly ease your hurt or loneliness. But I would ask you to remember what Geoff would want of you:

> He would want you to be loving and true
> Strong and faithful, as was his love for you.
> Remember he chose you as the pearl
> To be the mother of his little girl.
>
> He would want you to keep your spirit bright
> And tuck in the boys; two kisses each night.
> "You must give the children, my love for me
> As I always gave my love all to thee."
>
> He would want you to keep, stored in your heart
> The promises made wh're near or apart.
> Let faith be your friend and God be your guide
> And Geoff will, forever, be by your side.
>
> He would want all of this from his sweet wife
> For that's why he loved all of his life.
> Oh my Diane, I'm sure Geoff would say
> Please keep the faith, teach the children to pray.

I will miss Geoff.

With love,
Ray

Amen

My son has gone today
To do what he thinks right,
And though he's far away
I know he'll proudly fight.

I miss this boy of mine
And hope that soon he'll send
A note to say he's fine,
And tell of this war's end.

But as the time goes bye,
My sense of fear grows more,
I know that some must die,
But not my boy, not this war!

And then came word one day
With a note that kindly said
He'll soon be on his way
And we're sorry that he's dead.

His body came today
To be back home again
No more to ever stray
He's with his Lord; Amen!

My Boy

In traveling thru my days,
I've had a friend or two.
Some have shared my ways,
But none as much as you.

You're the man of my pride,
And a joy as my friend.
You have stuck by my side,
You have helped me to mend.

Wherever you may be,
My love is always true.
For you are part of me,
And I am part of you.

No more than this to say,
But tell you of my joy.
That on this happy day,
I'm proud to say "My Boy".

The Help Of One

There lives a small and dark abode
That I visit now and then
It lies upon a twisted road
That hides its ugly face from men.

It's not a place I like to go
For the grounds are poorly done
And nothing good will ever grow
Because it lacks God's light and sun.

The tragic part about this home
Is the landlord's really me
I keep it hid and all alone
So none will ever, ever see.

Of course the place of which I speak
Is the corner where I find
That prejudice will sometimes sneak
And live within my life and mind.

I wish that I could paint this place
And make the in and out all new
And clean the yard and make more space
To let the light of God shine thru.

I know the things that must be done
Of paint and plants and moving sod
And most of all, the help of one,
The help of one, called God.

Inheritance

He made a gift for me
The man I call my dad
And it shall always be
The best of what he had.

It's not of stone or rock
That I could lose some day
It isn't land or stock
That man can take away.

It isn't coin or gold
Nor anything to touch
And though it's very old
To me it means so much.

A gift for every day
Is what he made you see
A path along life's way
Is what he gave to me.

Dear Daddy

I know you can't respond
To my whisper in your ear
For I know you're now beyond
The words that men can hear.
And I know you cannot see
The pain upon my face
That says you're gone from me
Beyond this earthly place.
And I know you cannot say
The words I long to keep
For your lips are sealed today
In this, your final sleep.

Yet I recall those many years
You listened with your being
And how you calmed my many fears
With faith, that eyes could not be seeing.
And I recall when I was weak
The strength in me you showed
Not with words that you would speak,
But with love that freely flowed.
And I remember each silent walk
When we'd wander through the pine
And even though we didn't talk
Our thoughts would still entwine.

I know our eyes and ears and speech
Are ne'er to meet again on earth
Yet love, I know, will span the breech
As it did before my birth.
For I know you loved me too
Before my life did start
So I know it must be true
That we can love apart.
I love you, daddy dear
And though you've gone away,
I'll keep your memory near
And love you everyday.

With Love - "Squirt"

My Son

My dad and I were friends
In a sort of distant way
I always had the time
But never did we play.

    He was always working
    On a thing or two
    Yet he always said
    "It's all my boy for you."

I learned a lot from dad
But not in lessons spoken
I learned you shouldn't cry
When the little promise is broken.

    He was always working
    On a thing or two
    Yet he always said
    "It's all my boy for you."

And as I grew unto a man
I thought his way was true.
For all that I was working for,
Would, my son, one day go to you.

He was always working
On a thing or two
Yet he always said
"It's all my boy for you."

Well, time has taught a lesson
My dad would sure agree
The best in life was not in work
But in the life he missed of me.

He was always working
On a thing or two
Yet he always said
"It's all my boy for you."

And so before I too, am damned
And before another day
I want to say I love you
And hear about your day.

For I will not be a workin'
On a thing or two –
"Cause all I really want
is to be a friend to you"

No Man Could Love You More

Oh once upon a time,
Before you were my wife
I felt that I was lost
And doomed for all my life.

But on the first of March
Before the dawn of spring
You told me of your love
And then my heart took wing.

Oh I have sailed the heights
Before, I'd never known
And all because of you
With all the love you've shown.

And when the spring arrived
Your flowers turned my way
And as I walked your path
It was a bright new day.

Oh I have seen the colors
Of God's most gracious land
And all because you gave
To me your loving hand.

Oh now it's summertime
And all of life is bright
I know that God looks down
And sees that all is right.

Oh happiness is mine
The best is always here
When you are by my side
And I can hold you near.

I know the fall of time
Must come to you and me
And yes, my dear, I know
The best is yet to be.

Oh I have known the best
With riches more than gold
For I have had your love
Thru all these years to hold.

The winter snow will come
As thus all seasons do
So let me tell you now
Of all my love for you.

Oh God I love you so
No man could love you more
'Tis you alone I love
And always shall adore.

And in a time to come
Will be a future life
And there in God's great land
Again you'll be my wife.

And I the wonders shall
Again in heaven see
When God does call your life
To be again with me.

I Have Gone To Fight

I have gone to fight a war
In some far distant land
And I know my blood may pour
Upon this foreign sand.
But it's not my death I fear
That makes my spirit weak
It's the noise from home I hear
That protesters chant and speak.

I have gone to fight a war
So all men may speak out
But one thing I abhor
Is the cowardly way they go about.
My spirit quakes at the sight
When protesters block the way
For it is very right
I stand and fight this day.

I have gone to fight a war
But one day I'll be back
And I want to find the door
Is firmly still in tact.
So protest then, if you must
But keep respect for me
For though you think your cause is just
The streets must still be free!

Where Else

Where else in all this world
Is a man so free to speak?
Where else a flag unfurled
That represents the weak?

Where else can freedom be
A place for everyone?
Where else can justice see
The rights of all as one?

Where else can protest earn
A corner place to shout?
Where else their flag to burn
Yet safely walk about?

Where else can worship see
The freedom of your choice?
And yet there still can be
A sole dissenting voice?

Where else but in the heart
Of the land I love this day
The whole and every part
It's called the U.S.A.

Success

Success is not for you
To give or take from me
Success is not a gift
Nor is it ever free.

Success is not the wealth
That man may pile high,
Success is not a rank
For which you bid and vie.

Success is what you earn
From God this very day,
It is a loving peace
For those who live His way.

Peace

'The war has come to end
And the peace must now begin.
It is the time to mend
The scars of man and war and sin.

The enemy is beat
And to rest, their arms have laid.
So let us not retreat
From the peace which must be made.

For if we fought this war,
And peace was not the final aim,
Than we, forever more,
Are doomed to feel its' bitter shame.

So put to rest the past
And lay sword with hate aside,
To make all freedom last
In honor of those who died.

Of Wealth and Things

Of riches that man may possess
Like titles or silver and gold
My life is so poor I confess
There's nothing that e'er could be sold.

Of money and land that I own
That mankind can measure me by
There isn't too much to be shown
No matter how hard I may try.

Of all these things I envy naught
For I have more than wealth can be
I have the prize that kings have sought
It is the love Christ gave to me.

Of all the things in give or take
The wealth that all His loving brings
Means more than all the riches make
In all this world of wealth and things.

Behold

The Lord looked down from heav'n one day
And saw how poorly man had done
So to His angels God did say,
I'm going to send to man, my son.

And so the Lord did send to earth
The Herald angel from above
To tell about the coming birth,
And sing to all of peace and love.

It came to pass just as foretold
That Christ, the Son, did walk with men;
And like a shepherd tends his fold,
He brought them back to God again.

Yet there were some of evil heir
That made this man a thorny ring
And as they it placed on His hair
They scoffed about this earthly king.

The evil thought that they could win
Thus sentenced Him to cross and death;
And so it was to conquer sin,
He had to forfeit His last breath.

And there upon a wooden cross
The world did hear His final view;
Said just before His conscious loss,
Forgive, they know not what they do.

But three days after death had come
He came to man on earth once more;
To let man know that He had won,
And ever conquered death's dark door.

Be thankful then, as men of old
Who fell on bended knee to pray;
When they heard the angels sing, behold!
The Lord our God hath risen this day.

Resting Place

When I have gone beyond the space
That measures man from day to day,
I wish that I could have a place
That restful e'er my soul can lay.

A place that those who knew me well,
Could come and visit for a while;
A place where love could seek and tell
And share with me their every trial.

I'd this place of rest to show
A path that's worn by you, dear friend;
A path that's ne'er too high or low
A path of love from end to end.

I'd like my final rest to be
A place where God can love me too
So if you would, the place for me,
Is deep within the heart of you.

So mark no place for me with stone,
Nor bring me plants with flowered lace.
For I will live with love alone
In this, my final resting place.

I Do

In all the words of poet's love
A verse I cannot find for thee;
A way that I can tell you of
The joy that you have brought to me.

Of all the love that e'er was said
They were the words thus spoke by you;
'Twas on the day that we were wed
You held my hand and said, "I Do."

Not Bought In A Store

'Twas the night before Christmas
And all through the towns
The registers were ringing
With the credit card sounds.

The debt was so great
It boggled the mind
Yet the charges kept coming
As each purchase was signed.

Ma Ma had just settled
With a sigh of relief
While I sorted bills
In a moment of grief.

Then in my mind
I heard a great crash
I knew in a moment
I'd run out of cash.

In the days that would follow
One thing would come true
My joy it would fade
The bills would come due.

I thought of a time
A time long ago
When love was the gift
We wanted to show.

'Twas the night before Christmas
And I knew at long last
The Christmas I longed for
Was deep in my past.

I looked at my wife
My children were near
And that's when I knew
That Christmas was here.

For all of the gifts
Which were under the tree
None could mean more
Than my family to me.
And so in the end
The gift which meant more
Came free from my God
And was not bought in a store.

WWJD

What would Jesus do
I've often heard it said
About decisions we must make
On how our life is led.

But in our hearts we know
Of just what He would do
So the question really is
Can Jesus live in you?

Can you forgive the wrong
As He's forgiven you?
So thus we know the answer
Of what would Jesus do?

Learning

When you were a child
We guided your way
On paths which you traveled
For most of each day.

We warned you of danger
We were sometimes your voice
When things were beyond
Your reason of choice.

Yet as you grew older
We slowly pulled back
And left you decisions
To make your own track.

The foundation was strong
Our teaching was done
And so to the world
We gave our young son.

We brought you to life
We helped you to grow
But that's not the end
There's more you must know.

Now you must learn
Of decisions you choose
Which are your winners
And which you should lose.

You must learn to be prudent
In all you elect
So judgment by others
Will win their respect.

And the hardest of lessons
You may have to earn
Is to take on a loss.
Yet profit and learn.

And so with love we lay
Our parental rights to rest
We wish that all goes well
And of course the very best.
Now go and face the world
Be brave in all you do
And remember that forever
We will always be loving you.

Remember Me

I must confess to you
The time is drawing neigh
When you, the child, will view
Me, the parent, with a sigh.

No longer will I hold
The wisdom you saw in me
For time has made me old
And soon, the child I will be.

The memories of today
Will be a loss for me
And thoughts of far away
Will be the only views I see.

In time you will become
A stranger I don't know
And I will sit and hum
A tune of long ago.

So make the song you hear
The one I sing this day
And let me hold you near
O remember me this way.

The Prayer Chain

There is an unseen chain
A chain of love and hope
It binds us all together
Far stronger than any rope.

Each link is held together
By a piece of angel hair
Woven by a saint
From each and every prayer.

Yet as each prayer is added
The chain does not grow longer
For each link is just a circle
That every prayer makes stronger.

And today the bond of caring
Has increased its strength again
For your name is in each prayer
And sent to God, Amen.

Farewell

Her eyes now closed to earth
Her body laid to sleep
Her soul now given birth
And sent to God to keep.

We pray your grief be blest
With guidance from above
That in her final rest
She knows of all your love.

A Prayer

Before I close my eyes this night
A prayer of thanks to God I send
For He did place within my sight
The loving grace of you, my friend.

And should my eyes ne'er see the day
My prayer of thanks to God shall wing,
For He did lead your path my way
And thus I've heard the angels sing.

A Mother's Gift

The love she gives her child
Begins before its' birth
A love so strong and giving
It lasts beyond her time on earth.

She denies her life's ambition
To do whatever must be done
To give and guide no matter what
To sacrifice what e'er may come.

This is love a mother's love
No stronger love will ever be
This is love a – mother's love
A gift for all the world to see.

And I am witness to this love
This mom, this mother of life
Has made me more than proud to claim
She is the mother, I call wife.

One Wish

If God would grant my longing
My desire would be just one –
That on this day of mothers
I'd get to see my son.

      I know the pain you feel
      Like mine is real and true –
      And I'm sorry for the past
      And the hurt I've given you.

If God would grant one wish
I'd make it one to last –
I'd wish for love anew
And forgiving of the past.

      Send me not presents wrapped
      But let this mother see –
      The only thing I need
      Is you truly still love me.

I Give Myself To You

I give myself to you
O Jesus Christ, my Lord;
And pray you me o'er
These troubled waters ford.

I need your guiding hand
To help me o'er my fear;
Please help me understand
The death of one so dear.

O help this child young
To understand this loss;
Remind him life's not done
For those who love the cross.

Now help us all we pray
To know this is our fate;
We all must pass this way
To enter heaven's gate.

Equality

All children are born
With God's holy grace
They know not of hate
Nor color of race
No prejudice is
Within their sweet heart
And hatred and fear
Is not the Lords part.

All that is noble
And all that is right
Is placed there by God
Before our first sight.
Yet as we become
The children of earth
We lose this great gift
God gave us at birth.

But if you would wish
To keep this gift true
Then do as your God
Would expect of just you
Treat all that you meet
With kindness of soul
Remember all man
Is part of one whole.

So child of God
This story believe
God did make Adam
And God did make Eve.
He made them to start
The mankind of earth
So thus we are all –
Equal by birth.

A Mother's Love

There is nothing more constant, nothing more sure
Nothing more loving, nothing more pure.
Nothing more lasting could possibly be
Than the bond of your birth which holds you to me.

There is no love, no love upon this earth
That exceeds beyond the bounds a mother earns in birth.
And there is no pain, no greater pain they say
When the love of that dear child, turns their heart away.

Listening From The Heart

Chatter, chatter, chatter
It never seemed to cease
And as each day went by
It seemed to ev'n increase.

Her voice became a sound
That ne'er he seemed to hear
Until one day she asked
Do you still love me dear?

It did not seem to him
A question she should ask
And so he went about
His mundane daily task.

But the silence was to her
A final crushing blow
For all she had to say
He didn't care to know.

She never asked again
Nor did she ever try
And though he noticed it
He never asked her why.

And as the years went by
Their house became a jail
Silence took its' place
As their words began to fail.

It really is too bad
Their life did go this way
Two people out of love
Until their dying day.

It seems they both forgot
That talking is an art
And speech is only good
When listening from the heart.

The Gardeners Of Eden

'Twas just before we went to bed
My wife of many years and I
Knelt down and to the Lord we said
Our prayer of thanks to God on high.

We thanked Him for the children sent
And all the love that they had shown
We thanked Him for the life thus lent
And all the beauty that we had known.

And when the reverent moment passed
I turned and kissed my wife goodnight
Not knowing then, it was the last,
My eyes would ever see that sight.

And as I shut my eyes that night
An angel came to me and said
Behold, your soul shall see the light
As from my body it was led.

My soul, thus naked, stood amidst
The heav'n I thought I'd never see
And there an angel read a list
Of what it called the life of me.

The angel reading soft and low
Spoke only of God's Eden place
About a man I didn't know
Who was a gardener of such grace.

The angel spoke of pruning things
And making plants grow straight and tall
It spoke of all the waterings
The gardener gave both big and small.

And as the angel turned away
I saw God's face before me light
And then I heard my God to say
This gardener's soul has lived just right.

God took my soul within His hand
And smiling said, you're welcome here
For in this place called Eden's land
The gardener is to God, most dear.

But Lord, my soul, did doth protest
It's not of me the angel read
Of all my gardens, at their best
There's not much good that can be said.

Behold the Lord then said to me
The angel speaks of gardening this,
And yet without my eyes to see
My soul could feel a garden's bliss.

O Lord, my God, I feel the heart
That in this garden, doth truly grow
But of this all, I had no part
As surely you and I both know.

But then my God gave earthly sight
To let me see the garden grown
And there in just the dim twilight
A gardener working all alone.

The Lord then said there once were two
But now the care is just by one
Alone, the gardener, then paused to view
The efforts of the work thus done.

The gardener then turned to face
The beauty of these flowers of life
I knew the what and where and place
And saw the gardener was my wife.

And then I knew the angel meant
That children were the plants we grew
For they were seeds that heaven sent
Who needed love and caring true.

The gardeners of God's Eden land
Are those who tend to life on earth
They shape and mold and lend a hand
To seeds that God gave to man by birth.

Printed in the United States
By Bookmasters